SECONDARY SCHOOL

Practice Papers in
MATHS

Age 10–11

ROBIN BROWN
Chartered Educational Psychologist

This book has been devised to improve your child's performance in selection examinations by providing practice in the types of test he or she is likely to encounter. It gives you the opportunity to work together towards success as you aim to gain a place at the school of your choice.

Advice on what you can do to help your child is given overleaf. At the centre of the book (pages 15–18) you will find a pull-out section containing answers for each paper and a test profile to chart your child's progress.

ISBN 0 340 65138 5

First published 1994

© 1994 Robin Brown

Printed in Great Britain for Hodder Children's Books, a division of Hodder Headline Plc, 338 Euston Road, London NW1 3BH

A CIP record is registered by and held at the British Library

Published exclusively for W H Smith by
Hodder Children's Books

TIPS FOR PARENTS

- The practice papers within this book offer your child the opportunity to experience questions similar to those that appear in assessment tests around the country. The tests have been designed to give your child an understanding of the principles involved and to increase self-confidence.

- 'Helpful Hints' are provided at the end of each practice paper. These offer guidance in answering particular types of questions and also recommend valuable study techniques. Encourage your child to cover over this section and only to look at it once the paper has been completed.

- Encourage the development of good exam practice such as:

  - looking over the paper quickly before starting

  - reading the questions carefully and answering exactly what is asked for

  - answering first the questions that you can answer and then the questions that you find difficult

  - planning your time carefully and working at a steady pace

  - staying calm and doing your best

- Allow 45 minutes for each practice paper.

- Do not allow the use of a calculator when answering any of the questions. Instead, encourage your child to use blank paper for rough working.

- Go through the completed paper with your child and discuss the 'Test Profile' questions on page 18.

- Encourage your child explain the reasons for giving a particular answer. By explaining the route to an answer, your child's understanding of that type of question will be strengthened and any mistakes will be learnt from. In practice papers such as these, learning how to improve performance is as important as the results in the preparation for future tests.

- Remember to make the tests enjoyable, to praise successes and to build up your child's confidence.

- Analyse the type of questions your child finds difficult and try to give more practice on these.

PRACTICE PAPER 1

Do not use a calculator

1 Add these:

a 5 6 4	**b** 7 9 3	**c** 5 7 6	**d** 8 4 6 3
1 2 3 +	1 2 4 +	4 1 5 +	1 7 3 7 +

2 Subtract these:

a 5 4 9
   1 2 6 –

b 7 6 4
   2 3 9 –

3 Divide these:

a 6 ⟌ 3 6 4 2   **b** 4 ⟌ 8 3 2

4

    a   One pen costs 56p.
             How much will four pens cost? _____

    b   How much change should you
             get from £3? _____

5 How many thirds are there in $1\frac{2}{3}$? _____

6 Divide these shapes into quarters and then shade in 1 ¹/₄:

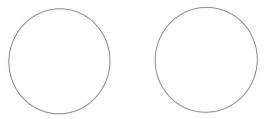

7 Jane walked for 3.4 km, jogged for 1.9 km and finally cycled for 8.2 km. How many kilometres did she travel altogether? (2 marks) _____

8 **a** Peter bought two pads of paper costing 42p each, two boxes of paper-clips costing 82p each and a box of pencils costing £1.12. How much did he pay altogether? (2 marks) _____

b How much change should he get from £5? (2 marks) _____

9 Draw a circle around the fraction in each box which is bigger:

| **a** ¹/₃ or ¹/₂ | **b** ³/₄ or ²/₃ | **c** ¹/₉ or ¹/₈ |

| **d** ¹/₂ or ¹/₄ | **e** ¹/₁ or ³/₄ |

10 Abdul woke up at 7.15 in the morning. Is this a.m. or p.m.? _____

11 Write these times as the times on the 24-hour clock of the video timer:

a 8.14 p.m. **b** 11.52 a.m.

12 The table shows the number of people who went on the roller-coaster at the Sierra Spectacular theme park over four days:

	THURSDAY	FRIDAY	SATURDAY	SUNDAY
ADULTS	25	a _____	122	120
CHILDREN	40	30	84	b _____

On Friday and Sunday, twice as many adults as children travelled on the roller-coaster. Use this information to fill in the gaps at **a** and **b**.

c How many children travelled on the roller-coaster on Saturday?   _____

d Which was the busiest day?   _____

e What was the total number of people on the roller-coaster on Thursday?   _____

f What was the total number of children travelling on the roller-coaster during the 4 days?   _____

13 Draw all the lines of symmetry on each shape.
(1 mark for each correct line of symmetry identified)

a

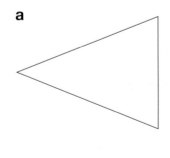

b

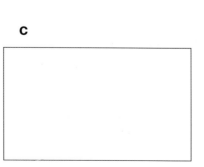

c

14 The diagram, which is not to scale, shows a plan of part of Annie's house.

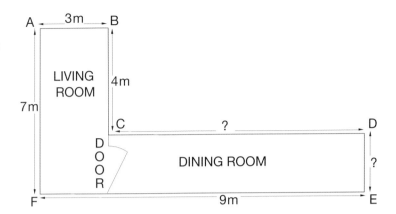

a What is the distance from C to D? _____

b What is the distance from D to E? _____

c What is the area of the living room? (2 marks) _____

d What is the area of the dining room? (2 marks) _____

e What is the perimeter of the *whole* area? (2 marks) _____

15 The following diagram shows the radar map of the runway and buildings at Munnit Airport. There is a Control Tower at T, a hangar at H, the start of the runway at S and the end of the runway at R. P is an aeroplane taxiing to the runway.

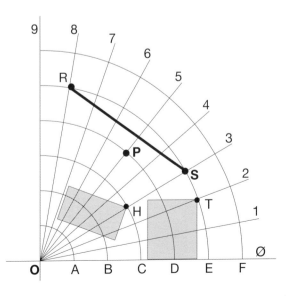

The position of the Control Tower at T can be described by the co-ordinates (E,2) because it is on the curve marked E and the line marked 2. In the same way describe the positions of

a R (,) **b** S (,)

c H (,) **d** P (,)

e Mark with a cross and the letter G the position of the fire-engine parked at (E,6).

f Mark with a cross and the letter W the position of the helicopter that landed at (C,7).

HELPFUL HINTS

4 **a** This is multiplication. If one costs 56p, four will cost 4 x 56p.

b To calculate the amount of change, you will need to subtract the answer for **a** from £3.

7 The total number of kilometres travelled can be found by adding the distances travelled by each method of transport or movement.

8 **a** Calculate the cost of each purchase separately.
e.g. two pads of paper at 42p each will be 2 x 42p; two boxes of pens at 82p will be 2 x 82p and the box of pencils is £1.12. Add each of these sub-totals together to give you the final total:
84p + £1.64 + £1.12.

b The change from £5 will be £5 minus the total found in **a**.

11 The times marked 'p.m.' are after 12 o'clock noon, so you add 12 hours to the figure of 8.14 to get the answer of 20.14. Remember, when changing a time to the 24-hour clock you always drop the 'a.m.' or 'p.m.'.

12 **a** and **b** Twice as many adults as children travelled on the roller-coaster, so you multiply the number of children by 2 to find the number of adults, or divide the number of adults by 2 to find the number of children.

d The busiest day is the day on which the total number of children and adults was greatest.

14 **a** The distance F to E is the same as A to B plus C to D because opposite sides of a rectangle are the same length. Therefore, if F to E is 9 m and A to B is 3 m, then C to D must be 9 m minus 3 m = 6 m.

b Similarly, to find the distance from D to E you calculate this as A to F (which is 7 m) minus B to C (which is 4 m).

c and **d** The area of a rectangle is found by multiplying the length by the breadth. For the living room this will be 3 m x 7 m and for the dining room 6 m x 3 m. Remember the units for the area will be in square metres, sometimes written as m^2 or sq.m.

e The perimeter is the distance around the boundary of an area, which can be found here by adding the distances A to B, B to C, C to D, D to E, E to F and F to A.

PRACTICE PAPER 2

Do not use a calculator

1 Add 349 to 786   _____

2 Multiply 943 by 7   _____

3 Add 2.34 and 4.87   _____

4 Multiply 56.2 by 0.4   _____

5 **a** The number I thought of is twice the number you get
        when you add 8 to 7. What number did I think of?   _____

   b I thought of another number and when I doubled it
        it came to 9 less than 37. What number did I think of?   _____

   c If I got out of bed at 7.25 a.m. and it took me
        50 minutes to get dressed, eat breakfast and be ready
        to leave the house, at what time was I ready to leave?   _____

   d Charlotte's birthday is on 28th August. Her sister's
        birthday is on 14th September. How many days after
        Charlotte's birthday is her sister's birthday?   _____

   e The classroom clock is 4 minutes fast. If it shows
        19 minutes past 2 in the afternoon, what is the correct
        time?   _____

   f Out of a class of 37, 19 children stayed in school,
        4 children travelled in Mrs Bunt's car, 3 in Mr Lake's car
        and the rest went in the school minibus when they went
        to the sports day. How many children travelled on
        the minibus?   _____

6 Circle the year in the brackets which is:

a 100 years after 1229   (1230, 1329, 2229, 1129)

b 1 year before 1879   (1881, 1779, 1878, 1979, 1880)

c 50 years before 1974   (1934, 1954, 1904, 1924, 1914)

d 2 years before 1501   (1599, 1503, 1499, 1502, 1603)

e 100 years after 1253   (1263, 1153, 1053, 1353, 1553)

7 Below is a timetable of the trains leaving Creek for various destinations:

Creek to:	Leaves Creek at:	Arrives at:
Torby	8.10 a.m.	10.20 a.m.
Sarbo	8.15 a.m.	9.55 a.m.
Marbed	8.40 a.m.	9.20 a.m.
Bewel	8.25 a.m.	9.55 a.m.

a How long does it take to travel from Creek to Sarbo?   _____

b How long does it take to travel from Creek to Marbed?   _____

c Which is the longest of the four journeys?   Creek to _____

d Which is the shortest of the four journeys?   Creek to _____

e How much longer does the train take to travel from
Creek to Sarbo than Creek to Bewel?   _____

f It takes 25 minutes to travel between Sarbo and Marbed.
If a train leaves Sarbo at 10.50 a.m., what time will it
arrive at Marbed?   _____

Nathan gets up at 7.15 a.m. but Surjit gets up 10 minutes
earlier. Anita gets up 15 minutes after Nathan.

g What time does Anita get up?   _____

h What time does Surjit get up?   _____

i If Nathan's bus is late and gets into Creek train station at
8.20 a.m., can he still catch the train to Bewel?   _____

8 Billy was 8 years old 3 years ago. His friend Joe is 3 years older than Billy. Mary is 6 years younger than Joe and Margaret is twice the age of Mary. How old are these children now?

a Margaret is _____   **b** Billy is _____

c Mary is _____   **d** Joe is _____

9 The radii of three circular birthday cakes are:

CAKE	RADIUS	BOX REQUIRED
A	15 cm	
B	8 cm	
C	12 cm	

The cakes fit into the special presentation boxes below with 1/2 cm gap between the cake and the side of the box. Write the number of the presentation box alongside the appropriate cake measurement above to identify the three boxes that need to be used. (3 marks)

10 Circle the correct description of each angle:

a	obtuse	right angle	acute	more than 90°
b	more than 180°	obtuse	acute	right angle
c	more than 90°	more than 180°	less than 90°	obtuse
d	obtuse	right angle	180°	acute	90°
e	90° 360° 100°	180° 45° 270°			

11 Change the order of the figures in the following numbers to make the largest number possible:

a 6732 _____ b 1947 _____ c 284 _____

d 8293 _____ e 4628 _____ f 2174 _____

12 Find the difference between the following pairs of numbers:

a 874 and 745 _____ b 937 and 27 _____

c 891 and 472 _____ d 8243 and 836 _____

13 Circle the smallest number in each line:

a 0.1   0.02   0.0009   0.3   0.001

b 8845   8754   8478   8574   8785

c 1/4   3/16   7/8   3/4   2/3   1/2

d 1.23   2.13   0.213   0.132   3.21   0.0312

11

HELPFUL HINTS

5 Follow the instructions carefully. For example, in **a**, 8 + 7 is 15, so twice the number is 15 x 2 = 30 which is the number I thought of.

d Remember, there are 31 days in August. Therefore count on from the 28th August to 14th September and this will give you 17 days.

e The clock is 4 minutes fast, so the correct time is 2 hours 19 minutes minus 4 minutes which is 2.15. Also, as it is in the afternoon it is 2.15 p.m.

8 Billy was 8 years old 3 years ago, so he is now 8 + 3 = 11 years of age.

Use this to work out the ages of the other children from the information given.

9 Remember, the radius is the distance from the centre of the circular cake to the side. So, the distance across cake **A** (the diameter) will be 15cm x 2 = 30 cm. If you then add 1/2 cm either side for the gap between the cake and the side of the box, the correct box for cake **A** must be:
30cm + 1/2 cm + 1/2 cm = 31 cm. This is box 2.

PRACTICE PAPER 3

Do not use a calculator

1 Write in the missing signs or numbers:

a 11 + 23 + ____ = 63

b 96 ____ 24 = 4

c ____ − 268 = 306

d 26 ____ 15 = 52 ____ 11   (1 mark only)

e 2 ____ 3 = 2/3

2 Multiply 576 by 28 _____	**3** Divide 4689 by 9 _____
4 Add 1/5 and 2/5 _____	**5** Add 3/4 and 3/4 _____

6 Each week for 3 weeks the teacher, Mr Patel, gave the class a spelling test. The marks each pupil got over the 3 weeks are given in the table below. The marks are out of 20:

NAME	WEEK 1	WEEK 2	WEEK 3
Vijay	14	14	20
Maria	7	16	16
Victoria	13	19	7
Robin	18	18	17
Suman	15	15	15

a Who scored the most marks in week 3? _____

b Who scored the most marks in week 2? _____

c Who scored the lowest mark in week 2? _____

d Which was Victoria's best week? _____

e　Which was Robin's worst week?　　　　　_____

f　Who got every question correct in one week?　　_____

g　Who had less than half marks in week 3?　　_____

h　Who found the test most difficult in week 1?　　_____

i　Who got exactly twice as many marks as Maria in week 1?　_____

j　Who was the most consistent in their scores?　　_____

k　What was Vijay's average score over the 3 weeks?　_____

l　What was the average score for the class in week 3?　_____

7　　**a**　17 cm = _____ mm　　**b**　1.4 m = _____ cm

　　　　c　3.25 km = _____ m　　**d**　560 g = _____ kg

　　　　e　4.7 litres = _____ ml　　**f**　3.6 kg = _____ g

8　Calculate the volume of each shape:

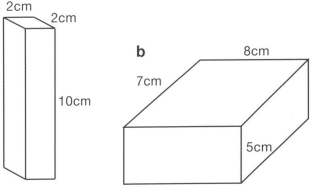
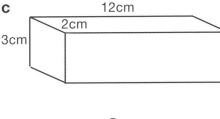

a　2cm　2cm　10cm

b　7cm　8cm　5cm

c　12cm　2cm　3cm

　　　　　　　　　a　_____

　　　　　　　　　b　_____

　　　　　　　　　c　_____

9　A tank is 6 m long and 4 m wide.

a　If the tank is filled with milk to a height of 8 m,
　　what volume of milk is in the tank?　　　　_____

b　If the tank is 11 m in height, what volume of the tank is
　　still empty?　　　　　　　　　　　　_____

ANSWERS

PRACTICE PAPER 1

1 a 687 **b** 917 **c** 991
d 10,200

2 a 423 **b** 525

3 a 607 **b** 208

4 a £2.24 **b** 76p

5 5

6

7 13.5 km (2 marks)

8 a £3.60 (2 marks)
b £1.40 (2 marks)

9 a $^1/_2$ **b** $^3/_4$ **c** $^1/_8$ **d** $^1/_2$
e $^1/_1$

10 a.m.

11 a 20.14 **b** 11.52

12 a 60 **b** 60 **c** 84
d Saturday **e** 65 **f** 214

13 a **b**

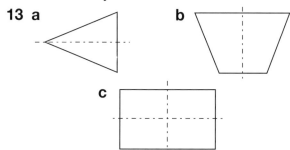

c

(1 mark for each correct line of
symmetry)

14 a 6 m **b** 3 m **c** 21 m^2
d 18 m^2 **e** 32 m
(2 marks each for **c**, **d**, and **e**)

15 a (E,8) **b** (E.3) **c** (C,3)
d (D,5)
e and **f**

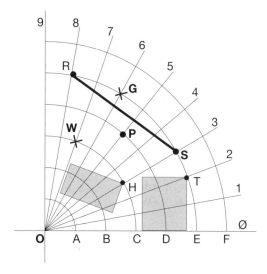

ANSWERS

PRACTICE PAPER 2

1 1135

2 6601

3 7.21

4 22.48

5 a 30   **b** 14   **c** 8.15 a.m.
d 17 days   **e** 2.15 p.m.
f 11 children

6 a 1329   **b** 1878   **c** 1924
d 1499   **e** 1353

7 a 1 hour 40 minutes
b 40 minutes   **c** Torby
d Marbed   **e** 10 minutes
f 11.15 a.m.   **g** 7.30 a.m.
h 7.05 a.m.   **i** yes

8 a 16 years   **b** 11 years
c 8 years   **d** 14 years

9 A 2   **B** 6   **C** 3

10 a acute   **b** right angle
c less than 90°   **d** obtuse
e 180°

11 a 7632   **b** 9741   **c** 842
d 9832   **e** 8642   **f** 7421

12 a 129   **b** 910   **c** 419
d 7407

13 a 0.0009   **b** 8478   **c** $3/16$
d 0.0312

PRACTICE PAPER 3

1 a 29   **b** ÷   **c** 574
d + and − (1 mark only)   **e** ÷

2 16,128

3 521

4 $3/5$

5 $1^1/_2$

6 a Vijay   **b** Victoria   **c** Vijay
d week 2   **e** week 3   **f** Vijay
g Victoria   **h** Maria   **i** Vijay
j Suman   **k** 16   **l** 15

7 a 170 mm   **b** 140 cm
c 3250 m   **d** 0.560 kg
e 4700 ml   **f** 3600 g

8 a 40 cm³   **b** 280cm³
c 72cm³

9 a 192 m³   **b** 72 m³

10 441 cm³

11 176 cm³

12 a 588 people   **b** £1470
c 84 people

13 a 36   **b** 12   **c** beach

14 a day 4   **b** day 7   **c** 7° C
d 20 °C   **e** day 3 and day 5
f day 4   **g** day 5 and day 6

15 a 25.4   **b** 365.2   **c** 5.921

ANSWERS

PRACTICE PAPER 4

1 a 9 **b** 69 **c** 24 **d** 15
  e 18 **f** 81

2 a $6/12$ **b** $4/6$ **c** $2/8$ **d** $10/12$
  e $4/10$

3 a Nicola **b** Steve and Andrew
  c 11 sweets **d** Nicola
  e 47 sweets

4 a 6 years **b** 8 years **c** 4 years
  d James

5 a The Bahamas **b** Brighton
  c The Bahamas
  d The Bahamas and Brighton
  e August **f** Rome **g** Brighton

6 a 0.5 m, 50 cm (2 marks)
  b 0.8 m, 80 cm (2 marks)

7 a 14 °C **b** 6 °C **c** 8 °C

8 a 60 k.p.h. **b** 20 km
  c 10 minutes **d** 25 minutes

9 a 60 km **b** 3 hours **c** 5 hours
  d 30 k.p.h.

10 a 3 children **b** 27 children

11 a £100 **b** £300 **c** £200
  d £1080

12 3416 g or 3.416 kg

13 37.46 kg

PRACTICE PAPER 5

1 a 2356 **b** 7.98 **c** $1 1/4$
  d 37.8 **e** 0.05 **f** $1/8$

2 5

3 £3.64

4 31 and 37 (1 mark)

5 19.29

6 a 8 **b** 4 **c** 9

7 a 12 **b** 36 **c** 52 **d** 4

8 a 6 **b** 14 **c** 20

9 a 25 **b** 64 **c** 4 **d** 7

10 a 25 **b** car **c** 25 **d** 75
  e $1/3$

11 a 44 m **b** 81 m^2 **c** 2 cans

12 79

13 9 minutes

14 a 10 hours 19 minutes
  b 7 minutes 16 seconds
  c 7 hours 15 minutes
  d 3 hours 20 minutes

15 200 g

16 £7.50

17 a 50 cans **b** 25 cans
  c

FRIDAY	■ ■ ■

  d 150 cans **e** 30 cans
  f 600 cans

18 a 4875 **b** $3/4$ **c** 0.9
  d 5.978

TEST PROFILE

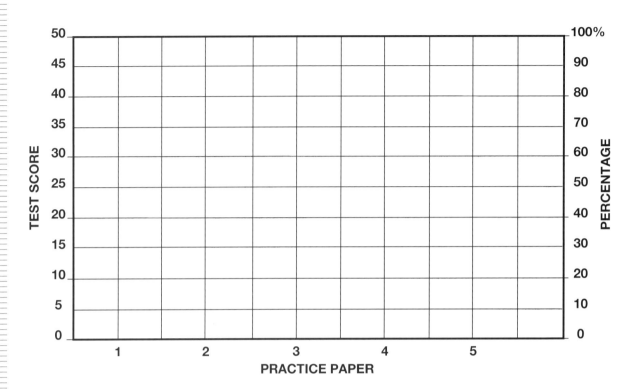

You can chart your progress on the above graph. Find your score on the left of the graph and then put a cross in the correct column depending upon the test that you have just completed. The right-hand side of the chart converts your score to a percentage (i.e. a score out of 100).

Look at the pattern of your progress and ask yourself some questions:

- Are there some types of questions at which you are better and some which you find difficult?

- What type of questions should you practise more of?

- Did you read the questions carefully?

- Did you misinterpret any questions?

- Did you answer exactly what was asked for?

- Did you forget how to do some questions?

- If you made a mistake on a question, do you know where you went wrong?

- Did you run out of time?

By answering questions like these, you can learn about yourself and it gives you clues about how you can improve.

10 A square-based carton measures 7 cm by 7 cm along the base sides and is 12 cm high. It is 3/4 full of orange juice. What is the volume of the orange juice in the carton? _____

11 A carton of a new drink measures 5 cm by 4 cm by 8 cm when it is full. As an opening 'special offer' the company make a carton which is 10% bigger. What volume of drink do you get in the 'special offer' carton? _____

12 The two sets of figures are the readings on a turnstile and record the number of people who passed across a bridge. The top reading was taken at the beginning of the week and the bottom reading at the end of the week:

| 1 4 0 8 4 SUNDAY |
| 1 4 6 7 2 SATURDAY |

a How many people passed through the turnstile that week? _____

b If each person was charged £2.50, how much money was collected by the end of the week? _____

c If the meter on the turnstile was read when the bridge was opened on Sunday morning and when it was closed on Saturday night, what was the average number of people who passed through the turnstile each day? _____

13 72 people were interviewed and asked how they had spent the last hour at the 'Great Fun Holiday Resort'. The pie chart displays their replies. If 12 people were in the cinema:

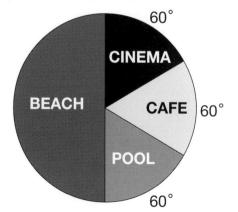

a How many were on the beach? _____

b How many were in the café? _____

c What was the most popular activity? _____

14 The graph records the maximum daily temperatures during Gemma's holiday. Use this information to answer the questions below:

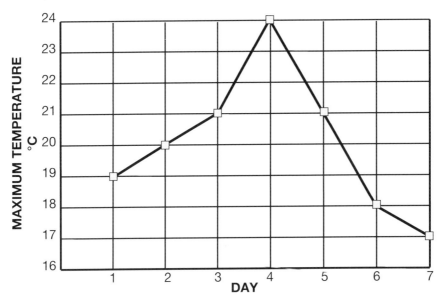

a Which day had the highest temperature? _____

b Which day had the lowest temperature? _____

c What was the difference in temperature between the hottest day and the coolest day? _____

d What was the average temperature for the 7 days? _____

e Which two days had the same temperature? _____

f Which days showed the sharpest increase in temperature? _____

g Which days showed the sharpest decrease in temperature? _____

15 Put a decimal point in the following numbers to make the figure 5 have a value of 5 units:

a   2 5 4

b   3 6 5 2

c   5 9 2 1

HELPFUL HINTS

6 If at first you do not understand a question, read it carefully and consider it from different angles. For example, in **j**, the person with the same mark each week is the pupil who was most consistent.

k Vijay's average score will be 14 + 14 + 20 = 48 divided by 3 (the number of weeks), so the answer will be 48 ÷ 3 = 16.

9 b If the tank is filled with milk to a height of 8 m and the tank is 11 m high, then the empty space is 11 m - 8 m = 3 m high. Therefore, the volume of the empty space is length x width (6 m x 4 m = 24 m^2) multiplied by the height of the empty space, i.e. 24 m^2 x 3 m = 72 m^3.

11 The volume of the carton is 5 cm x 4 cm x 8 cm = 160 cm^3. 10% of 160 cm^3 is 16 cm^3, so you get 160 cm^3 + 16 cm^3 = 176 cm^3 in the 'special offer' carton.

12 a Remember to subtract the smaller number from the larger number so the sum will be 14672 - 14084.

c To work out the average you need to divide the total number of people (588) by the number of days (7) to give the answer, i.e. 588 ÷ 7 = 84 people.

PRACTICE PAPER 4

Do not use a calculator

1 The patterns in these sequences follow regular rules.
Work out the rule and write in the missing number:

a 0   3   6   _____   12   15

b 93   87   81   75   _____   63   57

c 96   48   _____   12   6   3

d 5   6   8   11   _____   20   26

e 33   27   22   _____   15   13   12

f 3   9   27   _____   243   729

2 Circle the fraction in the brackets which is the same as
the fraction at the beginning of the line:

a 1/2   (3/5   4/6   6/12   6/8   3/9)

b 2/3   (4/8   4/12   4/10   2/4   4/6)

c 1/4   (3/6   2/8   2/6   3/9   4/12)

d 5/6   (10/14   4/8   10/12   12/14   3/9)

e 2/5   (3/10   8/12   4/12   4/6   4/10)

3 Steve has ten sweets, Nicola has twelve, Liz has nine and Sarah
has six. Andrew also went to the shop and bought ten sweets.

a Who has twice as many sweets as Sarah?   _____

b Which two children have the same number of sweets?   _____

c If Steve gave half his sweets to Sarah, how many would
she have then?   _____

d Who has the most sweets?   _____

e How many sweets do the children have altogether?   _____

22

4 James was 5 years old 3 years ago. His friend Ali is 2 years younger than him and Tim is half as old as James.

a   How old is Ali now?   _____

b   How old is James now?   _____

c   How old is Tim now?   _____

d   Who will be the oldest in 2 years' time.   _____

5 Use the chart of the average day- and night-time temperatures of three holiday resorts to answer the questions that visitors are asking the local travel agent.

RESORT	JULY		AUGUST		SEPTEMBER	
	DAY	NIGHT	DAY	NIGHT	DAY	NIGHT
THE BAHAMAS	31 °C	21 °C	31 °C	21 °C	29 °C	17 °C
ROME	30 °C	18 °C	28 °C	17 °C	28 °C	16 °C
BRIGHTON	20 °C	11 °C	21 °C	12 °C	19 °C	10 °C

a   Which resort has the highest daytime temperature?   _____

b   Which has the lowest night-time temperature in August?   _____

c   Which resort has an average night-time temperature above 20°C in July?   _____

d   Which resort has the same night-time temperature as the daytime temperature in another resort during the same month?   _____

e   Which month is this?   _____

f   Which resort has the same average daytime temperature in both August and September?   _____

g   Which is the coldest resort in September?   _____

6 This is part of a ruler.

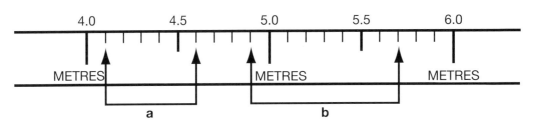

The length of line **a** is _____ m

or in centimetres _____ cm

The length of line **b** is _____ m

or in centimetres _____ cm

(4 marks)

7 What is the temperature on these thermometers?

a

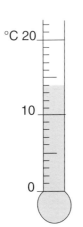

b

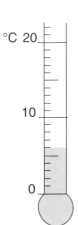

a _____

b _____

c What is the difference in temperature between **a** and **b**? _____

8   Use this graph of John's journey to answer the questions below.

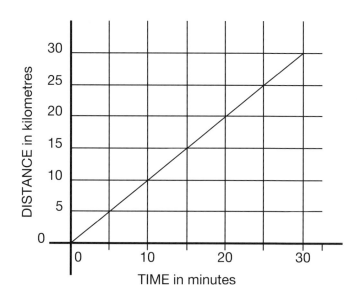

a   What is John's speed in kilometres/hour?   _____ k.p.h.

b   How far does John travel in 20 minutes?   _____ km

c   How long will it take John to travel 10 kilometres?   _____ minutes

d   How long will it take John to travel 25 kilometres?   _____ minutes

9   Complete the table below for each of Jenny's journeys. The first one is done for you:

SPEED	TIME	DISTANCE
6 k.p.h.	3 hours	18 km
30 k.p.h.	2 hours	**a** _____
10 k.p.h.	**b** _____	30 km
20 k.p.h.	**c** _____	100 km
d _____	6 hours	180 km

10 In Mrs Sharp's class there should be 30 children but 10% of them are away with flu.

    a How many children are absent with flu? _____

    b How many of the class are in school? _____

11 In the great 'bonanza' sale at Taylor's Department Store several items are being sold off. Work out the price you would pay for each item in the sale:

ORIGINAL PRICE £200 * 50% OFF * SALE PRICE:

ORIGINAL PRICE £400 * 25% OFF * SALE PRICE:

ORIGINAL PRICE £250 * 20% OFF * SALE PRICE:

HOLIDAYS GALORE!

ORIGINAL PRICE £1200 * 10% OFF * SALE PRICE: travel brochure

    a Picture

    _____

    b Watch

    _____

    c Table lamp

    _____

    d Holiday

    _____

12 A box of chocolates weights 427 g. What would 8 boxes weigh? _____

13 Two children weigh 72.24 kg. If one of the children weighs 34.78 kg, what does the other child weigh? _____

HELPFUL HINTS

4 Work out James's age first. James was 5 years old 3 years ago, so he must be 5 + 3 = 8 years old now. Then use this information to work out Ali's and Tim's ages.

   d James is the oldest now so he will still be the oldest in two years' time.

5 Make sure you answer exactly what is asked for. For example, in **f**, more than one resort has the same average daytime temperature over two months, but only Rome has this in both August and September.

8 From the graph you can see that John travels 30 kilometres in 30 minutes. Therefore, in 1 hour (60 minutes) he will travel 30 x 2 = 60 kilometres so his speed is 60 k.p.h.

9 Speed = Distance ÷ time so, in **d**, to find the speed you divide 180 kilometres by 6 hours (180 ÷ 6 = 30) which gives you 30 k.p.h.

If you want to find the distance travelled, you multiply the time of the journey by the speed. So, in **a**, the distance is 2 hours x 30 k.p.h. which gives the answer 60 kilometres.

11 A percentage is a fraction out of 100. Therefore, in **d**, 10 % of the original price of £1200 is $10/100$ or $1/10$ of £1200 which is £120. To work out the sale price you take £120 away from £1200 to give you the answer of £1080.

PRACTICE PAPER 5

Do not use a calculator

1 Calculate:

   a 589 × 4 = _____   **b** 4.81 + 3.17 = _____

   c $3/4 + 1/2$ = _____   **d** 6.3 × 6 = _____

   e 0.35 ÷ 7 = _____   **f** $1/2 \times 1/4$ = _____

2 How many sides has a pentagon? _____

3 If Delroy paid for something with a £5 note and he received £1.36 change, how much did the item cost? _____

4 What are the next two prime numbers after 29? (1 mark only) _____

5 Write 7.29 p.m. in the 24-hour clock. _____

6 Find the highest common factor (H.C.F.) of:

   a 16 and 24 _____

   b 12 and 20 _____

   c 18 and 27 _____

7 This diagram represents the responses when a group of people were asked if they liked tea or coffee.

   a How many people only like coffee? _____

   b How many people like tea? _____

   c How many people were interviewed? _____

   d How many people do not like tea or coffee? _____

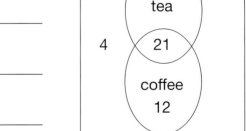

8 What is the lowest common multiple (L.C.M.) of:

a 2 and 3? _____

b 2 and 7? _____

c 2, 4 and 5? _____

9 What is

a the square of 5? _____   **b** the square of 8? _____

c $\sqrt{16}$? _____   **d** $\sqrt{49}$? _____

10 People entering a theatre were interviewed as part of a survey to find out how they had travelled there. The results are presented in the graph below:

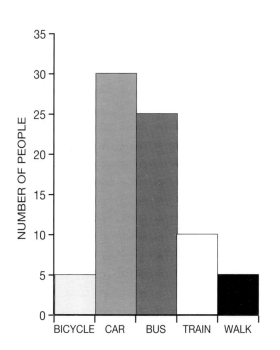

a How many people travelled to the theatre by bus? _____

b What was the most popular form of transport? _____

c How many more people travelled by car than walked? _____

d How many people were interviewed during the survey? _____

e What fraction of the total number of people interviewed travelled by bus? _____

11 Below is a plan of a room which has a wooden floor in need of revarnishing:

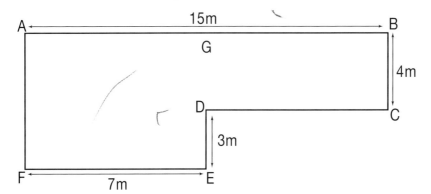

a What is the perimeter of the room?

_____

b What is the area of the floor?

_____

c A 2.5 litre can of varnish covers an area of approximately 45 m². How many cans of varnish will you need to revarnish this floor with one coat?

_____

12 How many 10 pence pieces make £7.90?

_____

13 A girl takes 14 minutes to walk to school. The school day starts at 8.45 a.m. One day she left the house at 20 minutes to 9. How late was she when she arrived at school?

_____

14

a Add:

hours	minutes
6	45
3	34 +

b Add:

minutes	seconds
2	54
4	22 +

c Subtract:

hours	minutes
9	46
2	31 −

d Subtract:

hours	minutes
8	12
4	52 −

15 7 bars of chocolate weigh 280 g. What is the weight of 5 bars? _____

16 If a person had £30 to share out equally between 4 people, how much would each person get? _____

17 The chart below shows the number of cans of drink sold from a vending machine at the swimming pool:

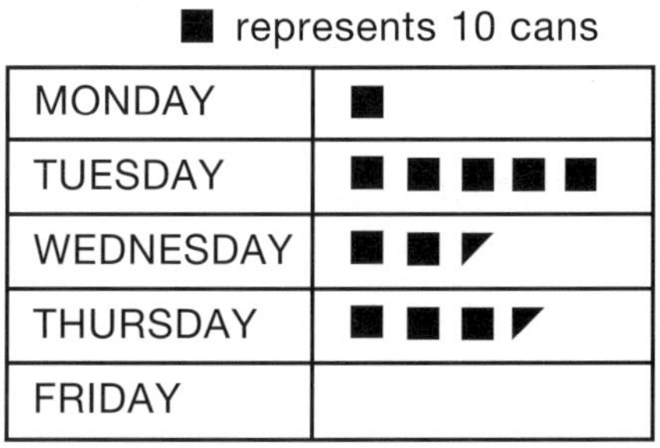

■ represents 10 cans

MONDAY	■
TUESDAY	■ ■ ■ ■ ■
WEDNESDAY	■ ■ ▶
THURSDAY	■ ■ ■ ▶
FRIDAY	

a How many cans were sold on Tuesday? _____

b How many cans were sold on Wednesday? _____

c On Friday 30 cans were sold. Show this on the chart. _____

d How many cans were sold during the whole week? _____

e What is the average number of cans sold each day? _____

f If this was a typical week how many cans would you expect to be sold over a 4 week period? _____

18 Circle the largest number in each line:

a 4785   4875   4578   4545   4758

b $\frac{1}{2}$ $\frac{3}{5}$ $\frac{3}{4}$ $\frac{1}{3}$ $\frac{4}{9}$ $\frac{5}{16}$

c 0.09   0.009   0.1   0.012   0.9

d 5.798   5.978   5.789   5.879   5.7

HELPFUL HINTS

6 The H.C.F. of two numbers is the largest number which is a factor of both of them, that is it will divide into both of them. For example, in **a**, 8 is the highest number which will divide into both 16 and 24.

8 The L.C.M. of two or three numbers is the lowest number that they will all divide into exactly. For example, in **c**, the L.C.M. of 2, 4 and 5 is 20.

10 b The most popular form of transport will be the one that scored the highest number of responses, which was the car with 30.

d To find out how many people were interviewed you must add up the total number of responses in each category.

e To find the fraction of those who travelled by bus you put the number who travelled by bus (25) as the numerator (the top line of the fraction) and the total number of people interviewed (75) as the denominator (the bottom line of the fraction). This gives a fraction of 25/75 which cancels down to 1/3.

11 a First work out the length of the sides that you are not given. For example, AF will be the same as BC + DE which is 4 m + 3 m = 7 m. The perimeter is found by adding the lengths of each side.

b One way to calculate the area of the floor is to work out the area of AGEF (7 m x 7 m = 49 m^2) and GBCD (8 m x 4 m = 32 m^2) and then add them together (49 m^2 + 32 m^2 = 81 m^2).

c One 2.5 litre can covers approximately 45 m^2, so you will need two cans to revarnish this floor with one coat.

14 Do not forget that these are calculations with hours and minutes or minutes and seconds, so take care and remember that there are 60 minutes in an hour and 60 seconds in a minute if you are borrowing or carrying.

15 7 bars weigh 280 g, so one bar weighs 280 g ÷ 7 = 40 g. Therefore, 5 bars weigh 5 x 40 g = 200 g.

17 b A whole square represents 10 cans, so half a square represents 5 cans. Therefore two and a half squares represents 10 + 10 + 5 = 25 cans, which is the number sold on Wednesday.

e The average number sold each week will be the total for the week (150) divided by the number of days (5) to give the answer 30 cans.

f If this was a typical week and 150 cans were sold, it is reasonable to expect that in 4 weeks 150 x 4 = 600 cans would be sold.

SECONDARY SCHOOL SELECTION

These **Practice Papers in Maths** are designed to improve your child's performance in selection examinations.

This book contains:

- test papers with answers
- advice for parents
- helpful hints on tackling the tests
- a test profile to chart your child's progress

Robin Brown is a Chartered Educational Psychologist. He has devised these papers to help parents and children work together towards success in gaining a place at their chosen school.

Practice Papers in this series:

English 10 – 11 *ISBN 0 340 65136 9*
English 11 – 12 *ISBN 0 340 65137 7*
Maths 10 – 11 *ISBN 0 340 65138 5*
Maths 11 – 12 *ISBN 0 340 65139 3*
Verbal Reasoning 10 – 11 *ISBN 0 340 67061 4*
Verbal Reasoning 11 – 12 *ISBN 0 340 67062 2*
Non-Verbal Reasoning 10 – 11 *ISBN 0 340 67063 0*
Non-Verbal Reasoning 11 – 12 *ISBN 0 340 67064 9*

Published exclusively for W H Smith

£2.99

ISBN 0-340-65138-5

00299

9 780340 651384